Super-Duper Shoes

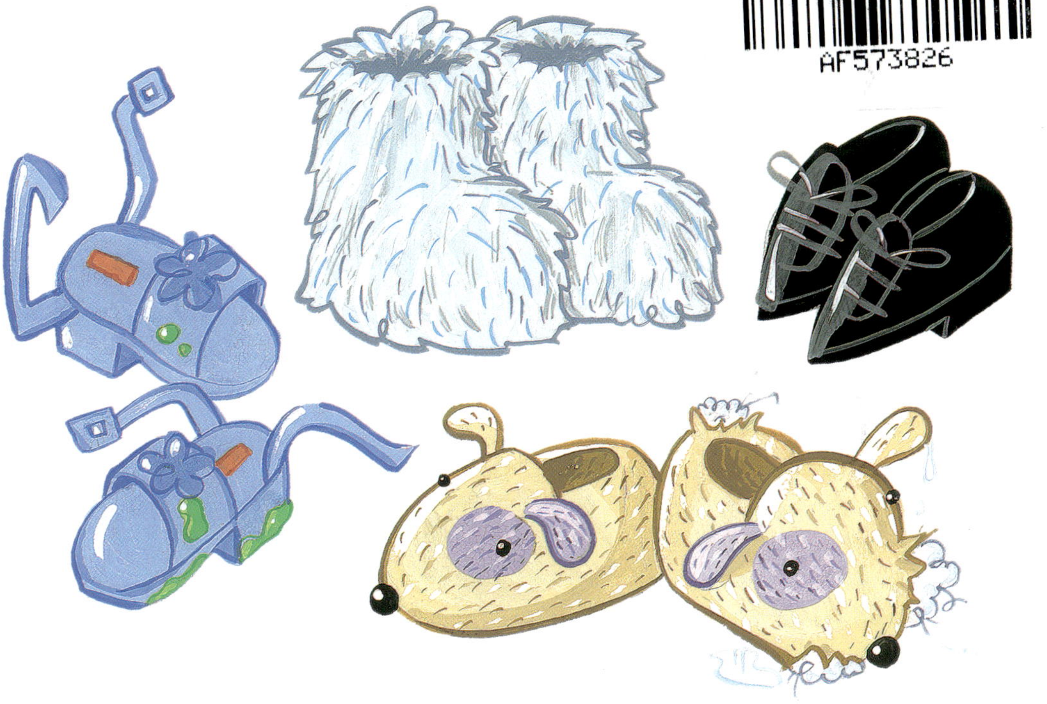

Tasha Pym

Illustrated by Melanie Sharp

I need some super-duper shoes for a super-duper surprise.

Snow boots are for building an igloo.

Snow boots won't do.

Lace-ups are for listening in lessons. (Especially when Miss Little says "Alice!" very loudly.)

School shoes won't do.

Slippers are for snuggling with
Snowy and snacking on the sofa.

Chewed slippers won't do.

Party shoes are for playing the princess.

Even party shoes won't do.

Oh no!

No more shoes . . .

I will just have to look ...

. . . in Mum's room!

Happy Birthday
Dad!
Happy
Birthday
Dad!